The Space Between Us

poems by

Anne Bower

Finishing Line Press
Georgetown, Kentucky

The Space Between Us

ACKNOWLEDGMENTS

"Age"—*Light Journal*, August 2017
"A Certain Contingency"—PoemCity, Montpelier, VT, April 2017
"Holding Pattern"—PoemTown, Randolph, VT, April 2017
"Red Heart"—*The Literary Nest*, April 2017
"Song for Serotonin"—first appeared on my website: www.annebower.com, Dec. 2016

For advice and inspiration, I thank poet Pam Ahlen. I also thank life-partner, James Rose, whose perception and steadfast support have made this effort and many others possible. And for creating this chapbook's beautiful cover, much gratitude goes to my son, Isaac Bower.

Publisher: Leah Maines
Editor: Christen Kincaid
Cover Art: Isaac Bower
Author Photo: James Rose
Cover Design: Elizabeth Maines McCleavy

Printed in the USA on acid-free paper.
Order online: www.finishinglinepress.com
              also available on amazon.com

Author inquiries and mail orders:
Finishing Line Press
P. O. Box 1626
Georgetown, Kentucky 40324
U. S. A.

Table of Contents

For my stepsister Nancy—whose honesty, humor, bravery, and joy in what pleasures remained as she succumbed to cancer

Attention

Picture frame, mat,
edge of canvas
or space around a sculpture
say—notice this
the artist making
strange and new
that ocean view, light's sheen on apples,
a hand's articulation, texture of steel or stone.

Space in the room between
our bodies as we move,
not empty but a force
frame and support
for mindful practice
and I notice how muscles pull
and settle the weight
how belly powers turn
exhale delivers push
and the room pushes back.

Fifth Grade Playground

I'd choreographed my moves
rehearsed fighting—
eyes narrowed to mimic tough,
knuckles ready to punch,
jaw clenched tight,
feet flat against playground blacktop,
convinced myself
this fierce facade would
banish the classroom bully.

But thin arms flailing
he charged
and when his fists struck
over and over
all my fakery
kindled to crimson fury,
blindly kicking, smacking, punching—
til he stumbled back,
ran.

Hours later,
after the teacher's lecture,
after the walk home past the
green grocer, the liquor store,
past brownstone buildings,
no sense of victory,
hatred and fear for the hatred I'd felt,
too aware of the danger I held.

Holding Pattern

The pilot's voice assures us
this holding pattern will end
in five minutes.

We of a certain age
know he's wrong.

We're always circling,
circling,
our fingers in brief touch
with peonies, shoelaces, liquid soap,
passport,
our arms embracing,
letting go,
hoping the circling fares well,
doubtful about the landing.

Pace

Deliberate steps
breathing into the moment
giving into each moment
living into each moment
slow steps allow air and space to enter

the quick step is only a step
hurry means fly into future—the meeting, office, store, train station

slow allows grass its green, September air its molecules of turning
leaves,
   allows all the bits and pieces of this moment
     and yes, what may unfold,
     remembering without haste
        to take the water bottle, the eggs for lunch, a change of clothes,
          the book we'll challenge
            sitting around the senior center's clichéd dropleaf table

Shrug off hurry, that worn, tight coat
Try the loose shawl of slow

A Certain Contingency

We build walls with dollars,
turn up the music,
boast of new cars, golf scores, stack-heeled shoes,
silk ties, three-star suppers, trips to Machu-Pichu.

But history has scarred us—
even those blind to the past.

That tough keloid
won't stretch and flex
but sometimes itches
warning
don't trust, don't believe, don't give,
don't even open the door.

Money

Finger-softened dollars in my wallet
blue plastic checkbook
   each month a pension
   brings automatic money
enough to fly eighteen hours to Hawaii
walk the black sands, tremble at spitting volcanos
enough to travel the fuschia-hedged
lanes of County Kerry
share paella in Nerja or Madrid
or buy my children cashmere
to warm their shoulders
in the cold of Albany, Madison, Pittsburgh,
or supple leather belts, hand-tooled
with intricate spirals and leaves.

They and I—why should we not
celebrate while we can—
taste, smell, touch,
grab the world's gifts.

I've spent and will spend to
buy storm windows, storm doors,
repairing this old house,
built two hundred thirty years ago
its floors uneven
grandkids' marbles
rolling west to east across
maple boards.

I save to cover the inevitable cancer,
angina, pneumonia costs,
the nurses, the tubes, shots,
the ambulance with its whirling light.

And still feel stingy.

The Ware Place

No wind, only the low hum
of the fan in the attic
carrying heat from the
wood stove crouching here in the kitchen
up through attic ductwork
pushing it down into the big living room—
simple mechanics

Hundreds of years ago
townfolk built this house
to coax a doctor into their woods
he, his vials and scalpels, wife
and children
fire place
wood cookstove
neighbors sparse

Some still call this
The Ware Place
though it's changed hands
a good dozen times
acreage pared from farm size
to just a lawn and garden

Snow swirls a flickering dance
coats the empty branches
covers neighbor's shorn pastures
sky a shadowed thick gray
steady tick of the clock
my pen whispers on unlined page

Legend has it the doctor
wrote a fine hand
served a while as town clerk

Neighbors

Pollen, road dust, humidity
swept away by early rain
sky-bowl clear now
sharp late September blue

Head cranked back, feet planted on the dirt road
arms outspread, palms up,
I'm pretending tree-ness
loving these enduring neighbors
their leaves so many tunes of green

The intricate oak a tall queen
fingering the air

The wide-spread maples attending,
large, small, crowding everywhere

Oval leaves of birch and its white bark
slim harlequins

Beech's skin soldier-thick,
gray, sturdy, solemn

Now the long gaze
beyond my road
to hills where
first hints of purple, red, yellow
tune up
for the big fall parade
that glory before
the trees stand humbled,
naked, cold, lichen-dappled in
every tone of brown,
roots beneath the snow
waiting

Hands

Hands that pull, lift, shape me
with a scientist's persistent curiosity
used to handling metal, stone
surprised by these muscles, tendons,
this yielding flesh
   learning to linger, tease, stray, hush.

Hands that unbutton, untie me
hold flowers or all of me
that for years held another hoping
for blossoming
   left with but a rough husk.

And in our moments together
even when we run ragged or
fall out of step,
miss cues, laugh or cry at wrong junctures
we find our bodies ringing anew
and sanctify all the places we visit
   all the places we touch.

Red Heart

"He would keep the rest where it belonged: in that tobacco tin buried in his chest where a red heart used to be. Its lid rusted shut" (Paul D. in Toni Morrison's *Beloved*)

The heart, that four-chambered box
of blood and muscle
we say is our center of feeling
though science credits the brain

The heart pumps
yet sometimes feels rusted shut
crouches, moans, weight of history
crushing—

iron bars, the hungry belly,
a ceiling low and dark,

weight of present
clutching apathy
despite knowledge, resolve, words

Surely something can pry off
this layered crust
some touch, generosity, need
can oil the hinges
release the fears that
close the box

Empathy

How many childhood hugs
does it take
to yield that easy smile
that loving sigh of sympathy
that brave unafraid
quiet ear open to
yelp of joy
grit of pain
moan of confusion?
To say—
I am as weak as you
and bend to your
struggle.

Star

I'm the star of this show
and you and you and you
emitting rays of hope, questions, joy,
anger, confusion

An eternity of rays pulsing
through space, crossing,
mixing

Passing years bring
some clarity—
I'm just one star
in this universe
where we always mingle
breathing each other
over and over

Now, now, now

Death snuggles up
purrs insistent message
now, now, now
low in the throat
more vibration than word
pet me, love me
and I promise this kindness
   each morning breath sharper
   each shower wetter
   each sip of coffee
   a better bitter
threatening, promising—
til one day
I bite.

Give and Take

Not sex
and yet
a bed—smooth, stainless steel

 he pushes, I yield
   thick red oak board
   slides through planer
   spiral cutters urge passage

my hands receive then heft the board
back across planer's top
where it rests

he turns the crank
   lowers cutters
   grasps and positions the plank anew
   flat on the bed

again it rolls into my hands

more passes   in and out
the grain coming clearer   cleaner   straighter

we dance through the work
intimacy of give and take
sawdust whirling through vacuum pipes
until the board achieves perfect 7/8ths inch thickness
and can rest to one side

and we go at it again

no words
  no moans
    no climax
though at hour's end when we stack the trimmed planks
we're both sighing

Ocean inside

Do you too walk about
with an ocean
inside
where notions
like big-eyed goldfish
or angelfish striped with blue
flash by
glimpsed just for a second

Other thoughts like giant tuna
linger, swirl, then disappear

And then there's one
like an octopus
reaching out with long
sensitive arms, suckers wet against your skin
clinging   grasping   holding fast

Postcard from Gold Branch State Park

We're in the land of
gap-mouthed fish mailboxes
scrubbed blond faces
long straight roads
and sandy soil
slash pine and saw palmetto
sweet tea and
cake-like corn bread.

A foreign land of many churches
but prayers don't save the lakes here
shrunken to mudpits.

Our own hearts shudder
constrict at the sight.

But yes, the weather's lovely.

Bleeding Pipes

She's worked out the heating system's journey
within their ranch style house—
analyzed, mapped
where air stalls hot water's circulation
back-pressure retarding heat.

She moves across carpet, wooden floor,
quietly, systematically,
the dog or a child trailing after,
stooping, pressing straightened paper clip against
the pin inside each air relief valve,
long thin hiss as air escapes
her own breath easing,
water free to flow
to fill the pipes again.

Her husband never asks to help,
never offers.
She'd say no if he did.

Garlic

Under late October clouds,
in three straight rows
we plant them deep,
each clove a quarter-moon
sheltered by garden soil,
eager roots pushing down
before the ground freezes.

We cover our plot—
clear, slitted plastic
stretched on wire hoops,
bury the plastic's edges
under shoveled earth,
admire this fragile quonset
hope it withstands
shifting winds,
snow's burden.

And wait the long Vermont winter—
through snow and shrinking days
freezing rain and ripping gusts

through days brightening
. . . snow thaw . . . ground thaw,

until plastic removed,
our sentinels of spring emerge,
yellow stalks
bright against the dark earth,
sing their way up and green,
leaf out, gain height,
stalks curling into scapes we clip,
sauté, share with friends,
while the plants, untroubled,
advance into summer's heat.

But stalks and narrow leaves
must wither, fade,
must sacrifice their power
to what's below ground
as each quarter-moon clove
transforms to fattened bulb.

We dig them up, let them dry,
ready them for storage,
praise color, size, type.
Now they're part of every soup, stew, sauce,
but the fattest cloves we'll plant again,
they wait in the cellar,
silent hoard of flavor.

Brown Hill

Soaring over some unnamed black dirt road
down the crest of Brown Hill, engine roaring,
lost. Past camps deserted, hayfields long mowed,
I'm stunned by another, silent soaring.

A huge gliding hawk spreads dark-fingered wings
rising up, up, into the bleached bone sky
carving the gray of coming rain. He brings
me found beauty. He will wheel, fly, wheel, fly

longing for the prey I've startled him from.
Riding currents with sure velocity
he waits, spiraling, for me to go home,
for me to remove mediocrity.

Beak down, he watches for my parting sign—
my intrusion spoiled his joy but made mine.

We

We is the proper term
twained or multiple
selves in one body
neither royal nor plural.
Admit it—you know it.
As in
You: one or two or many.
We: the same.

Twist the grammar
make it real—
We is home now:
Sitting, typing—
resentful, bored, edgy part,
calm, thoughtful, deliberate part,
coffee part; water part
(and single malt
and steaming broth).

One body perched on an exercise ball,
bouncing while seated,
eyes focused on computer screen,
room and window views peripheral,
slippered feet on the floor,
fingers on the keyboard,
selves and cells in constant swirl.

Swirl

Why deny
inner cry
to reach, plunge, swirl
refuse sigh
promote I
accept mad whirl
refuse shy
promote eye
images unfurl
doubts rise, die,
return, so sly
break pattern, kick door,
slam barefoot though snow
snap bare branch
rough twig every shade of brown, gray
words fail
fall

Some of us draw—

Some of us draw and paint,
pull pen, pencil or brush across paper,
board, canvas, wall
make known a dahlia,
a figure slumped on
a cracked subway seat,
newspaper under her arm,
ballerina caught mid-arabesque,
a pile of boxes
or root balls
or pure strokes and shapes.

> Some of us chisel, shape clay,
> collect and arrange old tools
> stray bones
> sticks, stones
> in figures and beasts
> two inches tall
> or twelve feet across
> to endure time's worries
> or rot in weather's vagaries
> maybe bridges, maybe mothers,
> maybe shapes unnamed.

Some of us note sound,
arrange melody and rhythm,
harmony and discord,
pull song from air,
the strings and keys,
bright horns,
tubes of black wood,
skins and sticks of drums.

Some of us pull muscle and
bones across a maple floor,
pavement, sand
in gestures and rhythm
shaping the air around
and within us
leaping, stomping,
tapping, whirling,
insisting
this is what bodies can do.

Some of us pull words
from the air
arrange them on paper
in weighted lines or
squared off paragraphs
love dialogue or plot.

And all any of us are doing, knowing our luck,
glad for this moment not to be pulling levers in a factory,
entering endless streams of data into a computer in a cubicle
in a windowless fluorescent-lit noisy space,
or endlessly packing tomatoes in crates?
We are opening, noticing

For a While

All the stories are stories
Someone's invention—
A singing voice, breathy pauses,
eyebrows flicking, fingers pointing,
listeners attentive;

Or minerals spread on walls
extolling the hunt, the capture,
the animals' power, the goddess's
fertile round body;

Or bodies prancing, whirling,
pushing and pulling, in the village,
on parade, on a stage,
an erotic tale of love, hate, victory;

Or small symbols carved and scribed,
scratched or tapped onto a surface,
gripping our minds
with what's called truth.

We love our stories—
want them to tell who we are
all we've done—
last after the body crumbles.
And they do
for a while.

Reflections on the Void

I
Dark beyond dark, endless dimension
without form
not zero
for that would shape it
a yawning void
nothing beyond nothing
ultimate potential.

II
A friend said
If we get permission from the state
we can be buried on our own land.
Imagine—
no shroud or box—
just dust to dust
feeding the earth.

III
My mother-in-law raged at death though ninety-four.
My step-mother, same age, said—okay.
My own mother at seventy four?
By the time I sat bedside, held her hand,
she was almost gone,
perhaps accepting that
the life now so narrowed
wasn't worth the effort,
yet her breath kept on,
phlegm-filled stifled efforts
until it didn't.

IV
No grand scheme
just circling flux
everything lasts
minutes, days, centuries,
tick of DNA, poem, painting,
compliments and curses,
recipes, inventions, habits, jokes
jewels and silver
a battered salad bowl
and history's pain
a shadow that follows
whether behind pressed lips
or in stories.

Song for Serotonin

We're a circle of six or ten or seventeen
    shifting and stepping through ritual warm-ups
        some move with grace, some struggle
    yet all sharing space, giving effort, chi—
to others, self, body, mind

No physical contact and yet
mere presence of others moving together
sends chemical messengers   dancing
                            and swaying
                through brain channels
            like bright-robed celebrants
                whirling through streets,
        tossing treats to the crowd,
free gifts, music, colors swirling,

 or like kindly relatives
hands on our shoulders
        bending close
looking into our eyes
    smiling softly
            saying
My . . . how you've grown!

After years of varied jobs (secretarial, cooking, running a flood control agency, grants writing, teaching art part-time), and after her children were grown, **Anne** began to write both fiction and poetry. That focus was derailed by pursuit of a Ph.D. and life in academia, where she taught American Literature and wrote books and articles about food and culture (*Recipes for Reading*, University of Massachusetts Press; *Reel Food*, Routledge; *Introduction to African American Foodway*s, University of Illinois Press).

After retiring from The Ohio State University she moved to rural Vermont where she teaches tai chi, gardens with partner Jim Rose and experiments with recipes, chairs the local Library Board of Trustees, visits with family whenever possible, and has time and quiet in which to write. Her poems often involve tai chi or food and the growing of it, but political concerns and issues of aging emerge too.

In 2013 Kattywompus Press published her chapbook, *Poems for Tai Chi Players*, and both PoemCity and PoemTown (events in Montpelier and Randolph VT) have included her poems in recent events. Her poems have appeared in *Light Journal, The Literary Nest*, and other publications.

www.ingramcontent.com/pod-product-compliance
Lightning Source LLC
LaVergne TN
LVHW021123080426
835510LV00021B/3295